I0772472

Immigration

Jackson B

IMMIGRATION

ISBN: 1983675466
ISBN-13: 978-1983675461

DEDICATION

Dedicated to western civilisation.

IMMIGRATION

CONTENTS

IMMIGRATION

Jackson B

ACKNOWLEDGMENTS

Thank you to those who have encouraged me to write this book and those who have offered suggestions to help improve the quality of the book.

1 INTRODUCTION

I've written this book because for the past year I've had an interest in the topic of immigration. This interest was initially sparked by Donald Trump's campaign to run for president, in which he proposed various things relating to immigration. The main items being a wall on the southern United States border and a temporary Muslim ban. My interest on this topic was further boosted by the 2017 election in New Zealand.

Immigration is the most important issue of our time. This can be simply justified by simply reading the news. In Europe, there is a refugee crisis. In New Zealand, there is a huge influx of immigrants which is drastically growing the population of the country. In the United States, there has been a lot of talk about illegal immigration.

A lot of immigrants are good people with no ill intentions. It's not their fault for taking advantage of a weak immigration system that seems prevalent in a lot of western countries.
It's not about establishing an ethnostate or promoting racist policies which would affect immigrants in a negative manner Immigration policy in the western world shouldn't be designed to protect a certain race. It should instead be

designed to protect the state and its citizens. The purpose of immigration should be to benefit everyone, rather than a certain class of people.

Immigrants aren't to blame for any of the problems caused like New Zealand's economy relying on migration to drive economic growth. For Europe being unable to cope with a sudden influx of refugees. For wages being depreciated as a result of mass immigration. Government policy is to blame for an over reliance on immigration as a whole. This has been done to make economic figures look good and to make the government look moral and caring on an international stage.

While the government gets praise for taking in refugees or for having impressive looking economic statistics at first glance. The reality is that a lot of hard-working, average citizens aren't doing so great. This morality and so-called economic growth isn't actually benefiting the working class.

The working class are the only kind of people I want to defend in this book. The working class are the main type of people being negatively affected by immigration. The reasons you will see throughout the book.

The purpose of this book is to encourage conversation about immigration as a whole. People need to start viewing immigration as something that needs to benefit the average person. This is in contrast to genuine arguments against immigration being smeared as racist and immigration being used to promote racialist policies. None of those things actually benefit the working class.

IMMIGRATION

2 REFUGEE CRISIS

Mainly caused by pointless American intervention in the Middle East which resulted in the rise of ISIS has sparked a major humanitarian crisis as a consequence. We typically know this as the refugee crisis, which has being nothing but trouble for Europe.

A lot of the issues caused with the refugee crisis is because of the sudden influx of migrants[1]. There's no quick and easy way to deal with these refugees. It's simply out of control. This has consequently resulted in poverty[2] with there being massive refugee camps -- especially at Calais. There's no cheap solution to giving these refugees decent accomodation, jobs, and other basic things we would take for granted[3].

A lot refugees don't have much of a future in their current state. They're not being encouraged to be entrepreneurs. They're not being taught any skills. Any attempts to do so are

---

[1] Foreign Policy, Study: About 1 Million Refugees Left in Limbo in Europe Through 2016

[2] European Commision, Refugees and internally displaced persons

[3] Independent, Syrian refugees will cost ten times more to care for in Europe than in neighboring countries

going to be expensive. By opening the floodgates, Europe has created a new underclass. Attempting to assimilate refugees is going to take generations to do[4], and at an extremely high cost.

The refugee crisis might have been solvable in Europe if regional players in the Middle East actually played their part. Saudi Arabia is the main country worth talking about. But while they're the main country, they're not the only ones that could have helped. United Arab Emirates[5], Qatar[6] and Kuwait [7] are some of the richest countries on the planet. They could have definitely pulled their weight as well in trying to mitigate the situation.

The reason why Saudi Arabia should do their part is because they have an empty refugee camp with air conditioning. They're also equipped with bathrooms and kitchen facilities. These are basic things that refugees in Europe have been missing out on ever since they've arrived there. This camp is called "City of Mena".[8]

Refugees that have gone to other Middle Eastern countries have had it much better than those who have gone to Europe. In Jordan, there is a refugee camp called "Zaatari". There, things that Europe needs to be doing is actually being done. Refugees are becoming entrepreneurs[9]. Refugees are also

---

[4] Al Jazeera America, Refugees Struggle to Assimilate in Germany

[5] Kjaleej Times, UAE's per capita GDP stays high

[6] Global Property Guide, GDP per Capita in Qatar

[7] Wikipedia, Economy of Kuwait

[8] Washington Times, Saudi Arabia has 100,000 air-conditioned tents sitteing empty, still won't take Syrian refugees

[9] BBC, Zaatari Syrian refugee camp fertile ground for small businesses

being taught in schools[10]. Not only that, their standard of living is much higher. Rather than living in tents, they're provided with cabins that have running water and electricity[11].

There has been some solutions to the refugee crisis in Europe that are important to mention. The only problem is that they're all actually horrible solutions for the working class.

In Germany, the Ministry of Employment has considered scrapping the minimum wage[12]. If this were ever put into practice, it would be terrible for the working class. A lot of working class people would be forced into worse and more expensive living conditions. This is all while being in competition to a million new people. This would definitely lower wages below a point that we consider a 'minimum', hence the name minimum wage.

The only people who would actually benefit from wages recessing are the elite[13]. These are the same people who live in their own gated communities far away from the realities of the real world. While the average person's wages would decrease, the rich would see a raise in their income.

Combine lower wages with less government investment as a result of there being less tax money. There could potentially be a lot of trouble in Germany if they ever thought about abolishing the minimum wage.

---

[10] Jordan Times, Eight new schools established in Zaatari camp

[11] Equal Times, The Zaatari camp: life in the middle of the desert

[12] Reuters, German conservatives seek minimum wage exceptions for refugees

[13] Business Insider, Profits Just Hit Another All-Time High, Wages Just HIt Another All-Time Low

The other so-called solution is the racialist approach. The advocates for this believe in establishing a white ethnostate. This would cause issues issues such as sanctions on the German economy, and capital flight. People simply wouldn't do business in Berlin anymore. After All, who would want to stay in a country that is going rogue?

Trying to establish an ethnostate would wreak havoc on Germany for many years. It would take decades to get back to the point they would be before in terms of respect, power, economic size and wages.

Under the ethnostate model, nobody would win. The upper-class would lose as they'd be forced to divest and flee. The working-class would lose as they wouldn't have jobs to go to. The ethnic government could theoretically try interfere with the economy, but that would only amplify the damage[14]. We all know that government involvement in the economy doesn't work as well.

Ethnostates also do not last very long. Apartheid South Africa only lasted 10 years when sanctions were levied on their country[15]. Nazi Germany only lasted 12 years. Rhodesia only lasted 14 years once they got UDI. If there's a recurring pattern happening here, it's that ethnostates do not last long. Though they each have their own reasons for not lasting very long.

All around, the ethnostate solution and the abolition of the minimum wage are both terrible ideas. These ideas should

---

[14] The Heritage Foundation, Government Intervention: A Threat to Economic Recovery

[15] Wikipedia, Disinvestment from South Africa

never seriously considered and proposed as a solution. They only would make the situation worse than what it already is.

The best solution solution to the refugee crisis from this point on is to incentivise refugees to go to the Middle East from Europe. Even if you reduced the amount of refugees by about 30%, that's still potentially 700,000 people that you don't have to worry about. This idea is proposed with the hidden implication that Europe will be letting in no more refugees.

IMMIGRATION

3 ILLEGAL IMMIGRATION TO THE UNITED STATES

In the United States, illegal immigration is a hot topic. Cracking down on it and deporting illegal immigrants is one of the Republican party major policies. The Democrats on the other hand are much more relaxed on the issue and are generally fine with giving amnesty to illegal immigrants.

When the 2016 United States election happened. The issue of illegal immigration was one of significance. This was ultimately because of Donald Trump and his proposal to build a wall on the United States-Mexico border. This sparked a lot of conversation about illegal immigration.

The main thing that it brought forward for me, doing research into the topic is how much illegal immigration can have a negative effect on wages[16]. There's no denying illegal immigrants are hard workers. But they have a negative effect on wages.
Illegal immigrants are working, doing jobs for significantly

---

[16] Federation for American Immigration Reform, Illegal Aliens Taking U.S. Jobs

lower rates than what their legal counterparts are doing. Not only that, they're not paying any taxes even though they're clearly benefiting from being in the United States. They use publicly-owned infrastructure to advertise their services. They also use public infrastructure each time they drink water or need to use sewage services. These people are getting all the spoils without any of the payment.

The Republican Party aren't the greatest party in the world, but on the topic of immigration they're the saviours of the working class. When they propose ideas like incentivising illegal immigrants to go home and reapply legally[17] this is a great way to raise wages for American workers.

Republicans are typically correct on illegal immigration. It is illegal. Those who do it should go home. By not having people working for half the rate that the average person might, then wages will go up. This is great for the working class.

Another Republican solution to illegal immigration is stopping the source of it. This is the wall that was proposed by Donald Trump in the 2016 election. Having a wall would make enforcing border laws easier[18]. It would create jobs[19]. It would also subjugate the working class to less competition, hence driving up wages.

Those aren't the only benefits. In terms of border security, this would be a one-time solution. You only need to build the

---

[17] Wikipedia, Self-deportation

[18] NPR, Head Of Border Patrol Union Weighs In On Trump's Wall Plans

[19] Bloomberg, Trump's Wall with Mexico - How many jobs would building a wall create?

wall once. This would save money on repairing the existence fences. It would also create a standard barrier rather than having multiple fences, barriers and sometimes even what would appear to be markers at random locations[20] which can be easily avoided, broken into and easily defeated[21]. A wall would be a challenge to defeat[22] no matter how far you're willing to go to try and overcome it.

Another area where money would be saved by building a wall is by not having to spend $100 billion on illegal immigration every year[23]. A $10-20 billion one-time solution could save up to $1 trillion over the course of a decade. Considering America's massive debt, they need to start coming up with other affordable and common sense solutions to other issues that they have that would save trillions.

---

[20] Avant News, Mexican Border Fence Comes Up Short

[21] NBC News, Here's What the U.S.-Mexico Border Looks Like Before Trump's Wall

[22] Daily Mail Online, Sessions: Border wall could make illegal crossings zero

[23] Federation for American Immigration Reform, The Cost of Illegal Immigration to US Taxpayers

IMMIGRATION

4 REFUGEE SITUATION IN NEW ZEALAND

Europe isn't the only area that has to take in their share of refugees. New Zealand, out of all places, still has to take in refugees despite it being not being a country that is close to the Middle Eastern conundrum at all.

New Zealand takes in 750 refugees a year[24]. Only 750. I would prefer 0. During the 2017 New Zealand election no party ran on keeping the status quo (at the very least) on refugees. All parties, in one form or another, advocated for an increase in refugee intake. The amount that they wanted to bring in was a figure that vastly fluctuated depending on who you were looking at.

National, Labour and NZ First all advocated for a doubling of the refugee quota to 1,500[25].

The Green party, on the other hand, advocated for a substantial increase to 5,000[26]. This is a 6 fold increase. It's

---

[24] Immigration New Zealand, Refugee and protection

[25] Whaleoil Media, What they promised and what we got: The refugee quota

[26] Green Party of Aotearoa New Zealand, Green Party to welcome 5,000 refugees to New Zealand

also an idea which clearly hasn't been thought out properly. It doesn't put the working class of our country first. This is the opposite. This is globalism at its worst form.

Those are just the amount of refugees we take in. The costs are also astronomically wasteful when you consider that we only take in 750 refugees.

According to an NBR article, the government spends about $81k per refugee when they come here.[27] This is estimated to be a total of $20 million when all added up. $81k per person is unsustainable if we want to increase our quota and it also doesn't help many people in the grand scheme of things.

Imagine if we followed through with the Greens policy of increasing refugee intake to 5,000. At a cost of $81k, that's $405 million per year. Over the course of 10 years, we'd have 50,000 more mouths to feed and we would have spent $4 billion.

New Zealand currently has a housing shortage, especially in the city areas.[28] This has caused rents and the price of houses to shoot up in a ridiculous manner.[29] This will be discussed later in the book. But a $4 billion investment over 10 years in housing would be better for the country as a whole rather than letting in a few refugees.

New Zealand should take in no refugees. That doesn't mean we can't do our part to help solve this crisis. If it's about

---

[27] The National Business Review, NZ to take 600 Syrian refugees on top of quota - at a cost of $48.8m

[28] NZ Herald, MBIE figures show nationwide housing shortage of 71,000

[29] NZ Herald, Brace yourself: Auckland rents are rising

helping people, we should seek to help the most people we can in this situation. By letting in 750 people into our country, we're not really helping anyone in the grand scheme of things except for 750 people out of millions in need.

The money that we spend on refugees ($20 million at the least) should be redirected to helping charities instead. $20 million could feed a lot of people in refugee camps for a long time. According to Unite for Sight, it only costs $50 a year to feed a school-aged girl for a year.[30] Feeding 400,000 school girls for a year would do more to help people in that situation rather than only spending an extravagant amount on a select few of refugees.

This is the type of common sense we need. This idea helps 533x more people than our current efforts. On top of that, it shows New Zealand's status as a soft power on the world stage. Not only would we be saving money, we would also look good for it in the process. That would be impressive PR.

---

[30] Unite for Sight, Fighting Hunger

IMMIGRATION

5 LOW-SKILLED IMMIGRATION IN NEW ZEALAND

For a long time now, New Zealand has had a weak immigration policy that has encouraged people of all types to come here. We've especially seen this in the past 4-5 years where net migration figures have been up to 72k.[31] On top of that, there has been reports that this figure was an underrepresentation of what was actually going on.[32] We could have up to 80k immigrants coming in, net.

What incentive does the government have to cut immigration though? It's one of the main drivers of our economy.[33] The key driver for us achieving 3-4% growth, one of the highest in the developed world[34] has been because of immigration.

Despite GDP growth being 3-4% at first glances, it's actually

---

[31] Interest, Statistics NZ figures show the lowest net migration gain for a September month since 2014

[32] **Newshub, Statistics NZ finds immigration statistics underestimated**

[33] Stuff, New Zealand's economic growth driven almost exclusively by rising population

[34] Beehive, Third highest growth rate in OECD

much lower when you look at it per capita. According to some calculations, using TradingEconomics as a source, our GDP per capita growth is only 1%.[35][36] That's terrible and pathetic growth, no matter how you would try and look at it.

People wonder why social investment looks weak. It's because it **is** weak. There's no real growth to allow to spend in a liberal manner. Our hospitals are full[37]. Our schools aren't being taught by anyone.[38] Our housing stock is full.[39] We're seriously in trouble if we don't do more to unlock the potential of our country.

Low-skilled immigration is driving up rents.[40] People are already struggling enough as it is. It's as simple as the demand is greater than the supply when it comes to housing in New Zealand -- yet nobody is proposing the common sense solution: cutting immigration. Any party therefore that advocates for low-skilled immigration cannot be a party for the common man.

Putting New Zealand second has made Kiwis miss out on having thousands of dollars more. If GDP per capita rose at 2%, we would have thousands of dollars more in the economy per individual. That would be literally double what we've gained in the past few years, especially of National rule. If we put ourselves first, we wouldn't have to deal with high house

---

[35] TradingEconomics, New Zealand GDP per capita | 1977-2018

[36] $(36842/36191) = 1\%$

[37] NZ Herald, Middlemore Hospital full: Patients told 'go elsewhere' or wait at least eight hours

[38] Newshub, Auckland primary teacher shortage worst in 30 years

[39] Newshub, NZ's homeless the worst in OECD by far

[40] Newshub, Tenants warned to brace themselves for record rents around the country

prices, wages being so low, hospitals being full and so on. Our country would be much better off regardless of how you look at it if we just put ourselves first.

Anyone with a brain would realise that we don't need all of these low-skilled immigrants in New Zealand. We need to reduce low-skilled immigration to 0. We do not need anymore low-skilled immigrants. That doesn't mean we should in favour of deporting immigrants that have already come here legally. Doing such a thing would also be terrible for our economy, and subsequently the working class.

We've already seen in multiple instances of how low-skilled immigrants are being exploited by our standards.[41] They're being paid well below minimum wage and they're unaware of their rights as a worker.[42] This is taking away jobs from Kiwis who are completely able to do them. The government not doing anything about low-skilled immigration is hurting both Kiwis and the immigrants.

The argument that low-skilled immigrants do the jobs Kiwis, or any other country's citizens don't want to do is a big lie. This argument is bad for the Kiwi worker when you think about it. That's because if there's a job position that's easily being filled up, that means there's more supply (workers) than demand (employers). This naturally means that wages will go down, or stay at minimum wage levels at the very least.

New Zealanders aren't lazy people. Our whole welfare state is designed towards getting you employed as soon as possible.

---

[41] Immigration New Zealand, Fruit contractor faces migrant exploitation charges
[42] NZ Herald, Uncovered: Exploitation of migrant workers rife in NZ

We clearly value hard work in this society but it would be better if there was less supply of workers. If the employer actually needed a worker they would be incentivised to put up their wages, at their own will, to attract employees. This would be better for everyone. The businesses would get employment, the worker would earn more money and the government would also get its fair share of tax revenue as a result.

Our country's philosophy on the situation should be that immigrants should be doing jobs we can't do, rather than "don't want to do". This means that we don't need to bring in cleaners and maids. We should instead bring in doctors, lawyers and similar jobs that are simply out of reach for most Kiwis.

6 HIGH-SKILLED IMMIGRATION IN NEW ZEALAND

High-skilled immigrants are the type of people we need in our country. They bring skills, capital[43] and most importantly they're not in competition with the average Kiwi. High-skilled immigration is the only type of immigration we truly need at this point in time.

High-skilled immigrants do the jobs that most of us are unable to do. A lot of us aren't doctors or teachers, the type of immigrants our country actually needs. This is important especially in this time of peril where hospitals are at their maximum capacity and where schools have all of their positions open and no teachers to educate kids.[44]

Highly-skilled immigrants are where the money's at. These are the types of people who are actually growing our economy at 3-4%. They're bringing in capital, starting businesses[45], making purchases in our economy. These are the immigrants who are helping enrich New Zealand the most. Not those with little to

---

[43] US News, Skilled Immigrants Bring Jobs, Capital, 'Unicorns' to U.S. Economy

[44] Radio New Zealand News, Teacher shortage: 'I've had no applicants'

[45] Toronto Region Immigrant Employment Council, The rise of the immigrant entrepreneur

no skills.

Unfortunately, a lot of high-skilled immigrants don't want to come here. They're much more interested in going to the United States or Australia. New Zealand is only a backup plan if they don't get into the big, more wealthier countries.[46] This is making our country miss out on hundreds of millions, if not billions of potential gains in the economy.

It seems our new Labour government has no interest in incentivising high-skilled immigration. One of the first things they did when they got into government was propose a law change would stop immigrants with wealth to come here.[47] I think letting in rich people is nothing but a gain for us. What do we have to lose letting in a few hundred millionaires? We only are set to gain from such a system. This is how Peter Thiel got his citizenship.[48]

If we had only high-skilled immigration we would have a much more prosperous country. Workers wouldn't be forced to compete for lower wages.[49] There'd also be more private investment since we would be targeting individuals to come here with specifically high wealth and skills.

If we only had high-skilled immigration, our net migration figures would be much more inline with what New Zealand First ran on during the election. Cutting immigration

---

[46] NZ Herald, John Roughan: New Zealand needs more people

[47] NZ Herald, Government considering law change to stop super-rich 'buying' citizenship

[48] The Guardian, New Zealand gave Peter Thiel citizenship after he spent just 12 days there

[49] Telegraph, Mass migration driving down wages offered to British jobseekers

significantly so that we only let in 10k migrants, net, each year.[50]

---

[50] Radio New Zealand News, NZ First loses battle on migrant numbers

IMMIGRATION

7 KIWIS MIGRATION TO AUSTRALIA

A lot of Kiwis have migrated to Australia. It's no secret that more Kiwis have gone to Australia than vice-versa. As of 2013, there were 650,000 Kiwis in Australia.[51] There is 62,000 Australians in New Zealand.[52] The Trans-Tasman Agreement has been a good deal for both sides. Though there have been times, especially in 2001, when Australia chipped away at Kiwis entitlement to welfare over there.[53]

Nonetheless, a lot of people are still happy to go to Australia even though they're not entitled to Centrelink programmes. A lot of Kiwis are still happy with agreement as Australia is a much more wealthier country,[54] with higher wages[55] and better living conditions than New Zealand.

Australians, on the other hand, are also free to come to New Zealand. Unlike Kiwis in Australia, Australians are eligible for

---

[51] Wikipedia, New Zealand Australians

[52] Te Ara Encyclopedia of New Zealand, Australians

[53] Stuff, New Zealanders in Australia are still treated like second-class citizens

[54] Analysis & Policy Observatory, Why is Australia so much richer than New Zealand?

[55] ABC News, Minimum wage: How does Australia compare to other countries?

WINZ.[56] This shouldn't be changed, except for extraordinary cases like free university tuition.

Both sides, when they migrate, feel like there's something to gain. The worst thing that could happen, especially to New Zealand is that agreement being cancelled. It would break hundreds of years of tradition of free-flow between the two countries.[57] It would be especially devastating for Kiwis, though it would definitely effects Australians as well.

Free-flow between Australia and New Zealand shows the special relationship between the two countries. Both countries do have something to gain from the deal.

There can always be improvements in the way Australians treat New Zealanders, especially in regards to welfare. The reality of the situation is that getting welfare isn't important. You shouldn't move to another country for the purpose of getting on the benefit. That's a bad deal for Australia. We shouldn't export our problems to other places.

The matter of the fact is that Kiwis are getting a good deal when they go to Australia. They're earning more money.[58] They live better. Living in Australia is cheaper.[59] Australia, compared to New Zealand, is a superior country when you compare the practical things.

Australians are the only people that shouldn't be affected by reducing low-skilled immigration to zero. They should be free

---

56 NZ Herald, Aussies access to welfare would not change, says Ardern

57 Wikipedia, Trans-Tasman Travel Arrangement

58 NZ Herald, Higher pay Australia's drawcard for Kiwis

59 Stuff, New Zealanders in Australia say Kiwis pay too much for food

to come to our country and vice-versa as they please. Keeping the Trans-Tasman agreement in tact is an important thing for New Zealand.

8 RECAPPING THE OVERALL EFFECTS

Middle Eastern countries, especially wealthy ones, should be doing more to help deal with the refugee crisis. Refugees that have gone to other Middle Eastern countries have had it much better than those who have gone to Europe. Refugees who have gone to other Middle Eastern countries have established semi-permanent communities[60]. They're entrepreneurs[61], their kids are being taught[62], and they have shelter. This is much better than how refugees in Europe and being treated.

Europe has created a new underclass. There's no easy to solution to this. The best Europe can do is close their borders and try and create incentives for refugees to leave. The costs of giving refugees jobs, accomodation and them an education will be substantial. [63]

Any racist plans against refugees will end up also being the demise of a country that implements it. It will be bad for the

---

[60] Oxfam International, Life in Zaatari refugee camp, Jordan's fourth biggest city

[61] BBC, Zaatari Syrian refugee camp fertile ground for small businesses

[62] Jordan Times, Eight new schools established in Zaatari camp

[63] Independent, Syrian refugees will cost ten times more to care for in Europe than in neighboring countries

working class and it's simply unsustainable. Countries that try discriminatory practices do not last. It will set the country back that tries racist policies back a few decades. That would destroy influence/power, respect and their economy. All important commodities in the modern world.

Donald Trump's plan to build a wall is the best thing to do when dealing with illegal immigration. It will save $1 trillion over the course of a decade.[64] It's a simple $20 billion solution that will create a challenge for illegal immigrants, no matter how far they try and go to get into the United States. Not having illegal immigrants compete with your job will protect United States citizens' jobs and improve their wages. Jobs will also be created as a result of the wall being built[65], which will be good for the economies near the border.

New Zealand should refuse to accept refugees. Instead, they should redirect the funds they spend on settling a mere figure of refugees into projects which will help much more people in the Middle East. This will show New Zealand's soft power on the global stage and make it look like it's doing it's share, despite it actually saving the country money. Potentially up to $4 billion over 10 years.

New Zealand should also refuse to accept low-skilled immigrants. We do not need to invite people to New Zealand to be janitors or a waitress. New Zealanders are perfectly capable of doing those kinds of jobs instead. If employers struggle to fund workers for any open fields, they should

---

[64] Federation for American Immigration Reform, The Cost of Illegal Immigration to US Taxpayers

[65] Bloomberg, Trump's Wall with Mexico - How many jobs would building a wall create?

improve the benefits of the job to attract New Zealand workers. This will be good for everyone.

New Zealand should only let in highly-skilled immigrants. These people have the most to offer our country in terms of capital they bring with them,[66] skills and their contribution to the economy.[67] An immigration system that targets skill and capital will help make New Zealand a much more prosperous country, which will benefit the working class.

New Zealand has a special relationship with Australia. The Trans-Tasman agreement that allows for free-flow of people between the two countries shouldn't be modified. All though it does appear unfair at some times, it benefits a lot of Kiwis and does Australians. It's not worth trying to constantly do an eye-for-eye approach to dealing with Australia. This will ultimately be the demise of the agreement, which if that were to happen, would put New Zealand at a disadvantage.

---

[66] US News, Skilled Immigrants Bring Jobs, Capital, 'Unicorns' to U.S. Economy

[67] Migration Policy Institution, The Contributions of High-Skilled Immigrants

Jackson B

9 THE ETHNOSTATE QUESTION

A small minority of people, typically named the "alt-right" support any form of immigration reform as long as it establishes an ethnostate.

A key feature of their form of immigration reform is preventing a certain race of people come into their country.

One faction is fine with their own racial group migrating though. All though this isn't an immigration system that completely cuts off people from entering the country, it doesn't incentivise the best. A person's race doesn't determine their individual skills. A lot of Africans who emigrate from Nigeria for instance are well-educated people. Under an immigration that values race over merit, an uneducated white person from the United Kingdom would be eligible to immigrate in the first place. Despite them carrying no value, whether it be in skills or capital.

That kind of system would distinctly put the working class at a disadvantage. If there's no requirement for skill, then they're automatically in competition with the working class. As we've gone over before in this book, low-skilled immigration drives down wages and drives up costs and decreases the availability of state services.

Another idea they have is to deport all people who are under a certain race. This would wreak havoc on the economy, which would hurt the working class the most. This would cause a lot of businesses to go under. This would destroy prosperity. Business confidence would be ruined and there would be capital flight and a brain drain, of all races.

Another faction flirts with the idea of stopping letting their own race emigrate. This is quite a silly idea though, because once people aren't allowed to emigrate, no new money can come into the economy. Repatriations of funds from emigrants back to their home one of the ways families become wealthy in third world countries. This is because of the massive cost of living differences between developed and undeveloped countries, the exchange rate, and also the availability of employment. Repatriation of funds would be a good potential revenue raiser for an ethnostate government. They don't seem to see that opportunity though.

A lot of advocates for the ethnostate also admit to not caring about the economy. That kind of thinking is extremely reckless will absolutely destroy them. South Africa had sanctions placed on them in the 1980's and a decade later they abolished apartheid. The economy is more important than the alt-right seems to think it is. A lot of people don't even care about the race of someone. They're more concerned about dinner on the table. A lot of advocates for an ethnostate do not seem to share these same priorities.

IMMIGRATION

10 NO BORDERS APPROACH?

Another group that exists is are advocates for no borders at all. People who argue for this are just as bad as those who argue for an ethnostate, though it does have its own reasons for being just as bad an idea.

A lot of advocates for no borders have typically been the more radical Libertarians. Though, a few progressives have also endorsed this idea.

A place where no borders have been tried is in Europe. This is well before the refugee crisis. There's free movement between all kinds of countries in EUrope, both poor and rich. This has created an influx of migrants from Eastern Europe countries into Western Europe. One of the prominent examples of this is the United Kingdom.[68]

As you can expect, not a lot of people left the United Kingdom and other more developed Western European countries towards Eastern Europe. The main trend is that

---

[68] The Guardian, Eastern European immigration to the UK: the facts

more people have come from Eastern Europe to Western Europe.

This flow of low-skilled immigrants into the UK has suppressed wages in the United Kingdom[69]. Outright open borders from them has been bad. It might allow them to holiday in Europe now with little to no restriction, but it's affected their way of life in a negative way. The price of housing in the United Kingdom is quite expensive depending on where you look.[70] The price of wages also doesn't reflect what's needed in particular areas as well.[71] It's mainly a problem in London and other cities, where a significant amount of the British population live.

For a lot of people in the United Kingdom, even trying to live in London is out of reach for a lot of people. Jobs are scarce.[72] Housing is expensive.[73] There's no actual incentive to live there.

The European Union's open door policy has been a contributor to London being expensive. British government also has a part to do with it as well with their own immigration policy of recklessly bringing in millions of immigrants when Blair was in charge.

If such a thing were to be implemented on a global scale, we would definitely see an exodus of people from poor, non-developed countries into developed areas. This would

---

[69] Express, Bank of England says immigration drives down wages

[70] Mirror Online, Are migrants driving house prices up?

[71] BBC News, One-fifth of jobs in London are low-paid

[72] The Guardian, UK unemployment: are there enough jobs to go round?

[73] The Telegraph, One in three home sellers in London are doubling their money

create poverty. There wouldn't be enough infrastructure or jobs to cope with it. An open-border policy would be terrible for the working-class.

Advocates for open borders are stupid and clearly haven't thought their positions. You need to have lines in the sand. Laws need to have their boundaries for where they're enforced. Confusion as to where laws should be enforced is ultimately what causes wars. A strong border with a clear line in the sand will prevent any conflict for the seeable future.

11 IMMIGRATION LOTTERY

An immigration lottery is the way the United States immigration system currently works. This was officially implemented in 1990.[74] It's a terrible system for dealing with immigration and the sooner the United States can get rid of it, the better.

The immigration lottery is a system that doesn't consider anything important that a country should look for in an immigrant. It doesn't ask what the immigrant can bring to the table. The only thing that a immigrant lottery considers important is having a bit of luck. That's an insane system.

A significant weakness in this programme was found in 2017. A recipient of this programme, Sayfullo Saipov, was fortunate enough to get into America.[75] He was only there for a few years before he committed a terrorist attack, killing 8 and injuring 11.[76] The immigration lottery doesn't take into account a person's abilities or health and in this case, you get a

---

[74] Wikipedia, Diversity Immigrant Visa

[75] Fox News, NYC terror attack suspect, Sayfullo Saipov, entered US through Diversity Visa Program

[76] Fortune, New York Truck Attack: 8 Dead, 11 Injured

nutter like Sayfullo.

The Republicans in 2017 made a significant push to try end the immigration lottery. They proposed replacing it with a merit-based, point system. A point-based system isn't anything new. It's already inplace in countries like Canada and Australia.

A point-based system is designed so that immigrants have to bring value to the country they're migrating to, otherwise they don't have a chance. This system benefits those in other countries who are skilled, but weren't lucky enough to come into America. because of the immigration lottery. This system puts those who are actually qualified to immigrate first.

It would be much more beneficial for the United States to make a switch to a merit-based immigration system as soon as possible. Making such a change would benefit the working-class. It would also bring much-needed value into the United States in the form of capital and skills. A merit-based system would be a great thing for the United States economy and immigrants.

12 GOING FORWARD

Going forward, it's important that we elect parties that endorse the idea of immigration reform and putting the nation first. In an era of globalisation and free trade, it's important that we protect the homebase.

Immigration is one of the only ways to protect workers from overseas competition. Protectionism economically does not work. It does the opposite of what it's intended to do, protect the workers and the industries of a country.

The entire purpose of immigration shouldn't be to lower wages. It should be engineered so that it improves the quality of services. Immigration should be helping a country's interests, not working against them.

As long as there's no immigration reform, real wages will continue to go fall. The population will be less secure. The government will be investing a significant amount into something that doesn't benefit most of the population. It's important that immigration reform is done as soon as possible, especially in the areas that have been mentioned throughout this book.

It's a shame that for the past 30 years we've neglected our citizens. Social investment could be significantly higher. People could have been earning more. In some instances, lives could have been saved. As long as we keep up with the status quo, nothing will change.

Fortunately, it looks like there could be some reform on the agenda:

* In New Zealand, there has been a new Labour-NZ First coalition government elected. Labour want to reduce immigration figures by 30,000 while NZ First wanted to reduce net immigration figures to 10,000. It's yet to be seen how far they'll be willing to go, but it's clear; the New Zealand government wants to reduce immigration.

* In the United States, the Republicans proposed merit-based immigration reform in 2017. Donald Trump is saying that he will sign the immigration reform bill proposed by the house. These factors combined will likely mean we will see the United States reform immigration in 2018.

* The United States are also cracking down on illegal immigration. There are eight wall prototypes that currently exist. The benefits of each wall is being evaluated by ICE and which wall will be used will be ultimately decided by Donald Trump.

* The United Kingdom has voted for Brexit. This will mean that there won't be any free flow of people between the United Kingdom and the Schengen Area. This will be a boon to British workers.

There is still a long way to go though. That's only the start of what needs to be done. All that is listed above aren't law yet. They're merely proposals at this point in time which means they're subject to change at anytime. Once we see one legislative victory for immigration, the rest of the world will have to follow in the end.

BIBILOGRAPHY

Foreign Policy, Study: About 1 Million Refugees Left in Limbo in Europe Through 2016

European Commision,   Refugees and internally displaced persons

Independent, Syrian refugees will cost ten times more to care for in Europe than in neighboring countries

Al Jazeera America, Refugees Struggle to Assimilate in Germany

Kjaleej Times, UAE's per capita GDP stays high

Global Property Guide, GDP per Capita in Qatar

Wikipedia, Economy of Kuwait

Washington Times, Saudi Arabia has 100,000 air-conditioned tents sitteing empty, still won't take Syrian refugees

IMMIGRATION

BBC, Zaatari Syrian refugee camp fertile ground for small businesses

Jordan Times, Eight new schools established in Zaatari camp

Equal Times, The Zaatari camp: life in the middle of the desert

Reuters, German conservatives seek minimum wage exceptions for refugees

Business Insider, Profits Just Hit Another All-Time High, Wages Just HIt Another All-Time Low

The Heritage Foundation, Government Intervention: A Threat to Economic Recovery

Wikipedia, Disinvestment from South Africa

Federation for American Immigration Reform, Illegal Aliens Taking U.S. Jobs

Wikipedia, Self-deportation

NPR, Head Of Border Patrol Union Weighs In On Trump's Wall Plans

Bloomberg, Trump's Wall with Mexico - How many jobs would building a wall create?

Avant News, Mexican Border Fence Comes Up Short

NBC News, Here's What the U.S.-Mexico Border Looks Like Before Trump's Wall

Daily Mail Online, Sessions: Border wall could make illegal crossings zero

Federation for American Immigration Reform, The Cost of Illegal Immigration to US Taxpayers

Immigration New Zealand, Refugee and protection

Whaleoil Media, What they promised and what we got: The refugee quota

Green Party of Aotearoa New Zealand, Green Party to welcome 5,000 refugees to New Zealand

The National Business Review, NZ to take 600 Syrian refugees on top of quota - at a cost of $48.8m

NZ Herald, MBIE figures show nationwide housing shortage of 71,000

NZ Herald, Brace yourself: Auckland rents are rising

Unite for Sight, Fighting Hunger

Interest, Statistics NZ figures show the lowest net migration gain for a September month since 2014

Stuff, New Zealand's economic growth driven almost exclusively by rising population

Beehive, Third highest growth rate in OECD

TradingEconomics, New Zealand GDP per capita | 1977-2018

Newshub, Statistics NZ finds immigration statistics underestimated

NZ Herald, Middlemore Hospital full: Patients told 'go elsewhere' or wait at least eight hours

Newshub, Auckland primary teacher shortage worst in 30 years

Newshub, NZ's homeless the worst in OECD - by far

Newshub, Tenants warned to brace themselves for record rents around the country

Immigration New Zealand, Fruit contractor faces migrant exploitation charges

NZ Herald, Uncovered: Exploitation of migrant workers rife in NZ

US News, Skilled Immigrants Bring Jobs, Capital, 'Unicorns' to U.S. Economy

Radio New Zealand News, Teacher shortage: 'I've had no applicants'

Toronto Region Immigrant Employment Council,

The rise of the immigrant entrepreneur

NZ Herald, John Roughan: New Zealand needs more people

NZ Herald, Government considering law change to stop super-rich 'buying' citizenship

The Guardian, New Zealand gave Peter Thiel citizenship after he spent just 12 days there

Telegraph, Mass migration driving down wages offered to British jobseekers

Wikipedia, New Zealand Australians

Te Ara Encyclopedia of New Zealand, Australians

Stuff, New Zealanders in Australia are still treated like second-class citizens

Analysis & Policy Observatory, Why is Australia so much richer than New Zealand?

ABC News, Minimum wage: How does Australia compare to other countries?

NZ Herald, Aussies access to welfare would not change, says Ardern

Wikipedia, Trans-Tasman Travel Arrangement

NZ Herald, Higher pay Australia's drawcard for

IMMIGRATION

Kiwis

Stuff, New Zealanders in Australia say Kiwis pay too much for food

Oxfam International, Life in Zaatari refugee camp, Jordan's fourth biggest city

Bloomberg, Trump's Wall with Mexico - How many jobs would building a wall create?

Migration Policy Institution, The Contributions of High-Skilled Immigrants

The Guardian, Eastern European immigration to the UK: the facts

Express, Bank of England says immigration drives down wages

Mirror Online, Are migrants driving house prices up?

BBC News, One-fifth of jobs in London are low-paid

The Guardian, UK unemployment: are there enough jobs to go round?

The Telegraph, One in three home sellers in London are doubling their money

Wikipedia, Diversity Immigrant Visa

Fox News, NYC terror attack suspect, Sayfullo

Saipov, entered US through Diversity Visa Program

Fortune, New York Truck Attack: 8 Dead, 11 Injured

NZ Initiative, The state of the New Zealand economy

Amanda Vickers, Winston Peters: Immigration & the NZ economy

Paul Henry, Peters: New migration figures 'a disaster'

ABOUT THE BOOK

Immigration is a book that focuses on key issues of the century. The book focuses on important matters such as the refugee crisis, low-skilled immigration, high-skilled immigration. It also addresses concerns about an ethnostate, having completely open borders, and the immigration lottery. The book is about advocating for a better quality life of citizens of western countries. There is a focus on how immigration hurts wages, allows for exploitation, and how people would be better off if they stayed at home rather than migrating. Sources from both left-wing and right-wing media have been used to help construct a main point: that most immigration isn't needed.